Grand Canyon
National Park

by Grace Hansen

abdopublishing.com

Published by Abdo Kids, a division of ABDO, P.O. Box 398166, Minneapolis, Minnesota 55439.

Printed in the United States of America, North Mankato, Minnesota.

102017

012018

Photo Credits: AP Images, iStock, Shutterstock

Production Contributors: Teddy Borth, Jennie Forsberg, Grace Hansen

Design Contributors: Dorothy Toth, Laura Mitchell

Publisher's Cataloging in Publication Data

Names: Hansen, Grace, author.

Title: Grand Canyon National Park / by Grace Hansen.

Description: Minneapolis, Minnesota : Abdo Kids, 2018. | Series: National Parks | Includes glossary, index and online resource (page 24).

Identifiers: LCCN 2017943143 | ISBN 9781532104343 (lib.bdg.) | ISBN 9781532105463 (ebook) | ISBN 9781532106026 (Read-to-me ebook)

Subjects: LCSH: Grand Canyon National Park (Ariz.)--Juvenile literature. | Arizona--Grand Canyon National Park--Juvenile literature. |National parks and reserves--Juvenile literature.

Classification: DDC 917.91--dc23

LC record available at https://lccn.loc.gov/2017943143

Table of Contents

Grand Canyon National Park

Grand Canyon National Park is in Arizona. The Grand Canyon became a national park in 1919. President Woodrow Wilson signed it into law.

5

The park is just over 1.2 million acres (485,622 ha). The canyon is nearly one mile (1.6 km) deep.

Weather

Different parts of the park experience different weather. This is because of the changes in **elevation**. The South Rim is at 7,000 feet (2,133 m). Summer evenings are cool. It can snow there in the winter.

Temperatures inside the canyon are much warmer. It can reach 120 degrees (49 °C) in the summer months!

Ecosystems

The park has several **ecosystems**. Like the weather, this is due to **elevation** changes.

Forests surround some of the canyon. Trees like pinyon pine and juniper grow there. Mule deer live in the park's forests. However they live in every area of the park.

The inner canyon is mostly desert. Cacti and **desert scrub** are common plants. Short-horned lizards live inside the canyon. So do rattlesnakes and other animals!

The Colorado River flows through the canyon. Different kinds of willow grow near it. Bluehead sucker fish are **native** and common in the river.

Amazing Condors

Flying above the canyon are California condors. These are one of the rarest birds in the world. Only the luckiest visitors will see one.

Fun Activities

Backpack overnight in the canyon

Take a mule ride around or into the canyon

Take a raft trip on the Colorado River

Walk the Trail of Time to learn about the canyon's rock layers

Glossary

desert scrub – multiple types of plants found in a certain desert habitat.

ecosystem – a community of living things, together with their environment.

elevation – the height above sea level.

native – original to.

Index

Visit abdokids.com and use this code to access crafts, games, videos, and more!